# Achiever's Guide to Success

By Bishop E. Bernard Jordan

ISBN 0-939241-10-2

The Achiever's Guide to Success

2nd Printing

# DEDICATION

This book is dedicated to my oldest daughter
Naomi Deborah Jordan, who will boldly carry the Word of the
Lord in her generation.

# *In Gratitude*

We'd like to give the following individuals a special thank you for their faithfulness and support in helping to make our dream come true:

*Yvonne Bascom & Family &*
    *Glynis E. McBean*
*Pastors Robert E. & Alma W. Bell III*
*Deborah Brower*
*Thelma Ward-Brown*
*Robert & Dina Davis*
*Annette Dean*
*Amber Estes &*
    *Felicia Fountain*
    *Cyndee Jemison*
    *Joyce Lewis*
*Peter & Helen Ferst*
*Pastor Bennie & Delores Fluellen*
*Adrienne Hays*
*Elder Fitzgerald A. King*
*Pastor Connie Miles*
*Prophetess Cherli Montgomery*
*James & Gertrude Taylor*
*Theresa Wedlock*
*James Wright*

Because of their generosity and obedience to the Spirit of God, we know that they have opened the door for miracles, and we believe that He shall cause the gems of wisdom that are contained within these pages to be made manifest in each of their lives, for the reward of the Lord is sure and addeth no sorrow!

In His Love and Service,
Bishop E. Bernard & Pastor Debra Jordan

# YOU WON'T BE SUCCESSFUL IN BUSINESS UNLESS YOU LOVE THE WORK THAT YOU DO.

*Ecclesiastes 3:22 "Wherefore I perceive that there is nothing better, than that a man should rejoice in his own works; for that is his portion: for who shall bring him to see what shall be after him?"*

## SUCCESS KEY #2

**A LOVE FOR WHAT YOU DO WILL SUSTAIN YOU AND PROVIDE ENTHUSIASM AND THE NECESSARY IMPETUS TO YOUR DRIVE FOR ACCOMPLISHMENT.**

*Ecclesiastes 5:18 Behold that which I have seen: it is good and comely for one to eat and to drink, and to enjoy the good of all his labour that he taketh under the sun all the days of his life, which God giveth him: for it is his portion.*

# A LACK OF LOVE WILL PRODUCE AN APATHETIC RESPONSE THAT WILL DRAIN YOU OF ENERGY AND ROB YOUR VISION.

*Ecclesiastes 2:10 ...for my heart rejoiced in all my labour: and this was my portion of all my labour.*

**SUCCESS KEY #4**

# IF YOU DON'T HAVE FUN IN YOUR UNCTION, THEN YOU ARE IN THE WRONG FUNCTION. YOUR CALLING MUST PRODUCE JOY.

*"Psalms 40:8 "I delight to do thy will, O my God: yea, thy law is within my heart."*

## YOU ARE A PRODUCT OF YOUR ENVIRONMENT.

*Proverbs 4:14-15 "Enter not into the path of the wicked, and go not in the way of evil men. Avoid it, pass not by it, turn from it and pass away."*

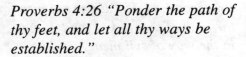

**SUCCESS KEY #6**

# IF YOU HAVE BEEN IN AN ENVIRONMENT CONDUCIVE TO GROWTH, YOU WILL GROW.

*Proverbs 4:26 "Ponder the path of thy feet, and let all thy ways be established."*

## SUCCESS KEY #7

# IF YOU HAVE BEEN IN THE COMPANY OF FOOLS, FOOLISHNESS WILL ERUPT.

*Proverbs 13:20 "He that walketh with wise men shall be wise: but a companion of fools shall be destroyed."*

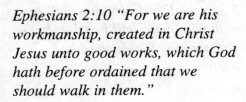

**SUCCESS KEY #8**

# WORK SHOULD BE LOVE THAT YOU MAKE VISIBLE.

*Ephesians 2:10 "For we are his workmanship, created in Christ Jesus unto good works, which God hath before ordained that we should walk in them."*

# WHEN YOU BECOME A PART OF ANYTHING, IT BECOMES A PART OF YOU.

*Psalms 90:17 "And let the beauty of the Lord our God be upon us: and establish thou the work of our hands upon us; yea, the work of our hands establish thou it."*

**SUCCESS KEY #10**

## YOUR LIFE IS A LIVING EXPRESSION OF THE USAGE OF YOUR MIND.

*Isaiah 26:3 "Thou wilt keep him in perfect peace whose mind is stayed on thee: because he trusteth in thee."*

# THE QUALITY OF YOUR LIFE IS AN INDICATION OF THE TYPE OF THOUGHTS THAT YOU THINK.

*Romans 12:3 "For I say, through the grace given unto me, to every man that is among you, not to think of himself more highly than he ought to think; but to think soberly, according as God hath dealt to every man the measure of faith."*

Bishop E. Bernard Jordan

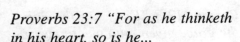
SUCCESS KEY #12

**SUCCESS IS A WITNESS TO THE LEVEL OF TRUTH YOU'VE MASTERED IN LIFE.**

*Proverbs 23:7 "For as he thinketh in his heart, so is he...*

## SUCCESS KEY #13

# FAITH IS A HIGHER LAW THAN REASONING.

*I Corinthians 2:5 "That your faith should not stand in the wisdom of men, but in the power of God."*

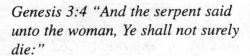

**SUCCESS KEY #14**

# REASONING CAN BE TAINTED WITH A LIE THAT APPEARS PALATABLE.

*Genesis 3:4 "And the serpent said unto the woman, Ye shall not surely die:"*

# FAITH, WHEN INCORPORATED WITH GOD'S WORD, CAN MAKE THE IMPOSSIBLE HIM-POSSIBLE!

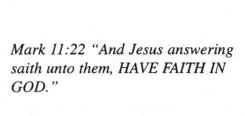

*Mark 11:22 "And Jesus answering saith unto them, HAVE FAITH IN GOD."*

## SUCCESS KEY #16

### FAITH IS THE CONTINUATION OF REASON, BUT IT IS ADVANCED.

*James 1:3-4 "Knowing this, that the trying of your faith worketh patience.*
*But let patience have her perfect work, that ye may be perfect and entire, wanting nothing."*

## SUCCESS KEY #17

# FAITH EXPANDS BEYOND THE BOUNDARIES OF REASON.

*James 2:20 "But wilt thou know, O vain man, that faith without works is dead?"*

## SUCCESS KEY #18

**REASON IS FORMULATED BY LAW AS MAN UNDERSTANDS IT, YET FAITH OPERATES BY A LAW DICTATED BY GOD, WHETHER UNDERSTOOD BY MAN OR NOT.**

*Matthew 16:8-12*
*"Which when Jesus perceived, he said unto them, O ye of little faith, why reason ye among yourselves, because ye have brought no bread? Do ye not yet understand, neither remember the five loaves of the five thousand, and how many baskets ye took up? Neither the seven loaves of the four thousand, and how many baskets ye took up? How is it that ye do not understand that I spake it not to you concerning bread, that ye should beware of the leaven of the Pharisees and the Sadducees? Then understood they how that he bade them not beware of the leaven of bread, but of the doctrine of the Pharisees and the Sadducees."*

# FAITH GIVES THE POWER TO BELIEVE AND THE POWER TO SEE.

*I Peter 1:7 "That the trial of your faith, being much more precious than of gold that perisheth, though it be tried with fire, might be found unto praise and honour and glory at the appearing of Jesus Christ:"*

Bishop E. Bernard Jordan

## SUCCESS KEY #20

# FAITH GIVES YOU THE ABILITY TO APPREHEND THE SUPERNATURAL.

*I John 5:4 "For whatsoever is born of God overcometh the world: and this is the victory that overcometh the world, even our faith."*

## SUCCESS KEY #21

# FAITH IS THE APPAREL OF YOUR DREAMS.

*Matthew 17:20 "...for verily I say unto you, If ye have faith as a grain of mustard seed, ye shall say unto this mountain, Remove hence to yonder place; and it shall remove; and nothing shall be impossible unto you."*

## SUCCESS KEY #22

# MONEY MUST BE UNDERSTOOD.

*Proverbs 13:7 "There is he that maketh himself rich, yet hath nothing: there is that maketh himself poor, yet hath great riches."*

# IF YOU DO NOT UNDERSTAND MONEY AND THE LAWS THAT GOVERN ITS ACQUISITION, YOU WILL NEVER APPREHEND ITS POSSESSION.

*Ecclesiastes 7:12 "For wisdom is a defence, and money is a defence: but the excellency of knowledge is, that wisdom giveth life to them that have it."*

## SUCCESS KEY #24

# MONEY IS THE SIGNAL AND BASIS FOR TRADE IN THE EARTH.

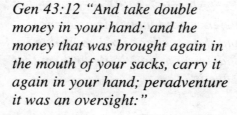

*Gen 43:12 "And take double money in your hand; and the money that was brought again in the mouth of your sacks, carry it again in your hand; peradventure it was an oversight:"*

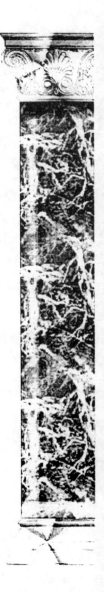

## MONEY POSSESSES AN INNATE POWER THAT SHOULD BE RESPECTED, BUT NOT WORSHIPPED.

*I Timothy 6:10 "For the love of money is the root of all evil: which while some coveted after, they have erred from the faith, and pierced themselves through with many sorrows."*

> **SUCCESS KEY #26**
>
> ## MONEY ANSWERS ALL THINGS, FOR ALL THINGS ARE ASKING QUESTIONS THAT REQUIRE AN ANSWER.

*Ecclesiastes 10:19 "A feast is made for laughter, and wine maketh merry: but money answereth all things.*

# MONEY TESTIFIES OF YOUR CHARACTER AND DEFINES YOUR MATURITY AND INTEGRITY.

*Proverbs 22:1 "A good name is rather to be chosen than great riches, and loving favour rather than silver or gold."*

**SUCCESS KEY #28**

# MONEY WILL LABEL YOU FOOLISH OR WISE.

*Proverbs 21:20 "There is treasure to be desired and oil in the dwelling of the wise, but a foolish man spendeth it up."*

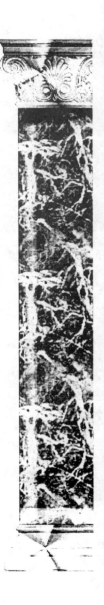

# YOUR WISDOM CAN BE SEEN THROUGH YOUR PROPER USE OR ABUSE OF THE LAWS OF MONEY.

*Proverbs 14:24 "The crown of the wise is their riches: but the foolishness of fools is folly."*

### SUCCESS KEY #30

# THE WORLD WORSHIPS MONEY.

*Luke 12:16-19*
*And he spake a parable unto them,*
*saying, The ground of a certain*
*rich man brought forth plentifully:*
*And he thought within himself, say-*
*ing, What shall I do, because I*
*have no room where to bestow my*
*fruits?*
*And he said, This will I do: I will*
*pull down my barns, and build*
*greater; and there will I bestow all*
*my fruits and my goods.*
*And I will say to my soul, Soul,*
*thou hast much goods laid up for*
*many years; take thine ease, eat,*
*drink, and be merry.*

# MONEY BECOMES A GOD TO THOSE WHO SEEK ITS POWER YET CANNOT DISCERN THE GOD OF THE POWER.

*Matthew 6:24 "No man can serve two masters: for either he will hate the one, and love the other; or else he will hold to the one and despise the other. Ye cannot serve god and mammon."*

### SUCCESS KEY #32

## MONEY IS NOT IRREPLACEABLE.

*Luke 9:3   And he said unto them, Take nothing for your journey, neither staves, nor scrip, neither bread, neither money; neither have two coats apiece.*

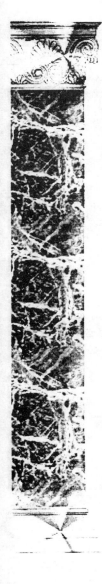

# WISDOM IS THE GENERATOR OF MONEY.

*1 Kin. 3:12-13 Behold, I have done according to thy words: lo, I have given thee a wise and an under-standing heart; so that there was none like thee before thee, neither after thee shall any arise like unto thee.*
*And I have also given thee that which thou hast not asked, both riches, and honour: so that there shall not be any among the kings like unto thee all thy days.*

**SUCCESS KEY #34**

# IF THERE IS A LACK OF WISDOM, THERE WILL BE A LACK OF MONEY.

*Prov. 26:13-14 The slothful man saith, There is a lion in the way; a lion is in the streets.*
*As the door turneth upon his hinges, so doth the slothful upon his bed.*

# IF THERE IS A HARVEST OF MONEY, IT DENOTES AN ABUNDANCE OF WISDOM.

*Proverbs 13:11 "Wealth gotten by vanity shall be diminished: but he that gathereth by labour shall increase."*

## SUCCESS KEY #36

# DO NOT ALLOW MONEY TO BECOME YOUR MASTER, FOR YOU WILL BECOME ENSLAVED TO ITS CONSUMPTION AND ACQUISITION.

*Matt. 6:24   No man can serve two masters: for either he will hate the one, and love the other; or else he will hold to the one, and despise the other. Ye cannot serve God and mammon.*

# SLAVE DRIVERS ARE CRUEL AND MERCILESS; AND THE SLAVERY TO MONEY WILL EXTRACT A CRUEL AND MERCILESS PRICE FROM THOSE THAT EMBRACE A COVETOUS MINDSET.

*Luke 16:13 "No servant can serve two masters: for either he will hate the one, and love the other; or else, he will hold to the one, and despise the other. Ye cannot serve God and mammon."*

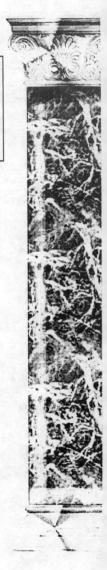

## SUCCESS KEY #38

# DOMINION WAS GIVEN TO MAN OVER ALL THINGS.

*Gen. 1:28   And God blessed them, and God said unto them, Be fruitful, and multiply, and replenish the earth, and subdue it: and have dominion over the fish of the sea, and over the fowl of the air, and over every living thing that moveth upon the earth.*

# MONEY IS A THING THAT MUST BE MASTERED, FOR MAN MUST DISPLAY THE DOMINION OF GOD IN THIS AREA.

*Luke 16:9 "And I say unto you, Make to yourselves friends of the mammon of unrighteousness; that, when ye fail, they may receive you into everlasting habitations."*

SUCCESS KEY #40

## MONEY SHOULD WORK TO ENLARGE YOUR HABITATION.

*Prov. 10:15 The rich man's wealth is his strong city: the destruction of the poor is their poverty.*

# MONEY IS A TOOL OF INCREASE. WHEN MANAGED WISELY, ITS PURPOSE IS TO BRING ENLARGEMENT INTO YOUR LIFE.

*Proverbs 10:15 "The rich man's wealth is his strong city: the destruction of the poor is their poverty."*

## SUCCESS KEY #42

# MONEY MUST BE GIVEN ITS FIELD OF EXPERTISE.

*Eccl. 6:11 Seeing there be many things that increase vanity, what is man the better?*

# MONEY IS DESIGNATED TO WORK FOR YOU, AND YOU MUST BE ABLE TO DISCERN THE FERTILITY OF THE FIELD IN WHICH IT IS PLACED.

*Ecclesiastes 5:13-14 "There is a sore evil which I have seen under the sun, namely riches, kept for the owners thereof to their hurt."*

## SUCCESS KEY #44

**MONEY WILL RUN FROM THOSE WHO ARE IGNORANT OF ITS LAWS, FOR THEY WILL VIOLATE THE LAWS THROUGH THEIR UNFAMILIARITY, AND INVITE POVERTY TO DINE AT THEIR TABLE.**

*Proverbs 23:5 "Wilt thou set thine eyes upon that which is not? for riches certainly make themselves wings; they fly away as an eagle toward heaven."*

# OBEDIENCE
## PRECIPITATES
## SUCCESS.

*Deut. 28:1  And it shall come to pass, if thou shalt hearken diligently unto the voice of the LORD thy God, to observe and to do all his commandments which I command thee this day, that the LORD thy God will set thee on high above all nations of the earth:*

## SUCCESS KEY #46

THE ATTEMPT TO
APPLY ANY OTHER LAW
BESIDES THE LAW OF
GOD IS A VIOLATION OF
HIS SOVEREIGN RULE,
AND WHAT WILL LOOK
LIKE SUCCESS WILL
ACTUALIZE FAILURE
WITHIN CERTAIN
FACETS OF LIFE.

*Deuteronomy 11:27 "A blessing, if
ye obey the commandments of the
Lord your God, which I command
you this day:"*

# OPPORTUNITY IS DRAWN TO PREPARATION AND WILL ATTRACT THE THING HOPED FOR, SINCE IT IS A DIMENSION OF ACTIVATED FAITH.

*Ecclesiastes 9:11 "I returned, and saw under the sun, that the race is not to the swift, nor the battle to the strong, neither yet bread to the wise, nor yet riches to men of understanding, nor yet favour to men of skill; but time and chance happeneth to them all."*

**SUCCESS KEY #48**

# THE LAWS OF GOD WERE GIVEN TO MAKE YOU PROSPER.

*1 John 2:2  And he is the propitiation for our sins: and not for ours only, but also for the sins of the whole world.*

# HIS LAWS ARE THE KEYS TO ALL THINGS PERTAINING TO LIFE AND GODLINESS.

*Joshua 1:6 "Be strong and of a good courage: for unto this people shalt thou divide for an inheritance the land, which I sware unto their fathers to give them."*

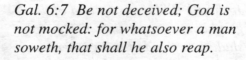

**SUCCESS KEY #50**

# SOW A SEED,
# REAP A HARVEST.

*Gal. 6:7  Be not deceived; God is not mocked: for whatsoever a man soweth, that shall he also reap.*

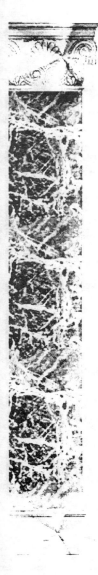

## SOWING AND REAPING IS AN IMMUTABLE LAW OF GOD THAT IS BUILT INTO THE UNIVERSE.

*Gen. 8:22 While the earth remaineth, seedtime and harvest, and cold and heat, and summer and winter, and day and night shall not cease.*

**SUCCESS KEY #52**

# THE DEGREE THAT YOU SOW WILL DETERMINE THE DEGREE THAT YOU'LL REAP.

*II Corinthians 9:6 "But this I say, He which soweth sparingly shall reap also sparingly; and he which soweth bountifully shall reap also bountifully."*

# TITHING WILL DETERMINE YOUR BLESSING OR YOUR CURSE.

*Mal. 3:9  Ye are cursed with a curse: for ye have robbed me, even this whole nation.*

## SUCCESS KEY #54

### TITHING IS A LAW THAT WILL VALIDATE YOUR LICENSE TO PROSPER.

*Malachi 3:8-10 "Will a man rob God? Yet ye have robbed me. But ye say, Wherein have we robbed thee? In tithes and offerings. Ye are cursed with a curse: for ye have robbed me, even this whole nation. Bring ye all the tithes into the storehouse, that there may be meat in mine house, and prove me now herewith, saith the Lord of hosts, if I will not open you the windows of heaven, and pour you out a blessing, that there shall not be room enough to receive it."*

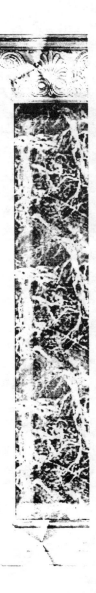

# THE FIRSTFRUITS BELONG TO GOD, NOT YOU!

*Leviticus 27:30 "And all the tithe of the land, whether of the seed of the land, or of the fruit of the tree, is the Lord's: It is holy unto the Lord."*

Bishop E. Bernard Jordan

**SUCCESS KEY #56**

# THAT WHICH BELONGS TO GOD IS DESTINED FOR CONSUMPTION.

*Nehemiah 10:38 "And the priest the son of Aaron shall be with the Levites, when the Levites take tithes: and the Levites shall bring up the tithe of tithes unto the house of our God, to the chambers, into the treasure house."*

**56**   ACHIEVER'S GUIDE TO SUCCESS

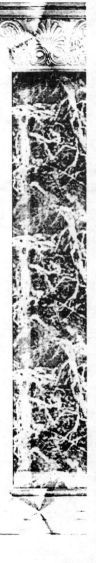

# GOD IS A CONSUMING FIRE.

*Hebrews 12:29 "For our God is a consuming fire."*

### SUCCESS KEY #58

# NEVER MIX GOD'S STUFF WITH YOUR STUFF!

*Joshua 7:11 "Israel hath sinned, and they have also transgressed my covenant which I commanded them: for they have taken of the accursed thing, and have also stolen, and dissembled also, and they have put it even among their own stuff."*

# THE BEAST AWAITS YOUR DISOBEDIENCE, FOR YOUR TRANSGRESSION BECOMES HIS LICENSE TO DEVOUR YOUR SUBSTANCE.

*Malachi 3:11 "And I will rebuke the devourer for your sakes, and he shall not destroy the fruits of your ground: neither shall your vine cast her fruit before the time in the field, saith the Lord of hosts."*

## SUCCESS KEY #60

**IF YOU DON'T GIVE THE TITHE TO GOD, THE DEVIL WILL CONSIDER IT AN OFFERING UNTO HIM, AND HE WILL FORCIBLY EXTRACT HIS HONORARIUM FROM YOUR LIFE.**

*Malachi 3:11 "And I will rebuke the devourer for your sakes, and he shall not destroy the fruits of your ground: neither shall your vine cast her fruit before the time in the field, saith the Lord of hosts."*

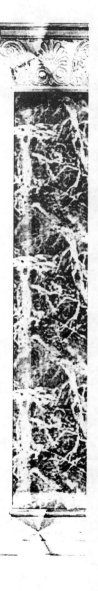

# YOUR FAITH IS CREATIVE.

Hebrews 11:1 "Now faith is the substance of things hoped for, the evidence of things not seen."

**SUCCESS KEY #62**

# GOD DESPISES THE OFFERING OF DISOBEDIENCE, FOR IT DISHONORS THE INHERENT INTEGRITY OF GOD, AND FLAUNTS OUR IRREVERENCE FOR HIS INSTRUCTIONS.

*Deuteronomy 8:19-20 "And it shall be, if thou do at all forget the Lord thy God, and walk after other gods, and serve them, and worship them, I testify against you this day that ye shall surely perish. As the nations which the Lord destroyeth before your face, so shall ye perish; because ye would not be obedient unto the voice of the Lord your God."*

# GOD WILL BLESS THE OFFERING OF OBEDIENCE, FOR IT DISPLAYS YOUR REVERENCE AND HONOR FOR GOD, AND WILL PROMPT THE RESPONSE OF HIS APPROVAL WHICH WILL MANIFEST THROUGH HIS BLESSINGS IN YOUR LIFE.

*Deuteronomy 5:32-33 "Ye shall observe to do therefore as the Lord your God hath commanded you: ye shall not turn aside to the right hand or to the left. Ye shall walk in all the ways which the Lord your God hath commanded you, that ye may live, and that it may be well with you, and that ye may prolong your days in the land which ye shall possess."*

## SUCCESS KEY #64

**IF YOU WANT WHAT YOU'VE NEVER HAD, THEN DO SOMETHING YOU'VE NEVER DONE!**

*Heb. 11:1 Now faith is the substance of things hoped for, the evidence of things not seen.*

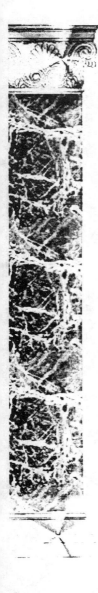
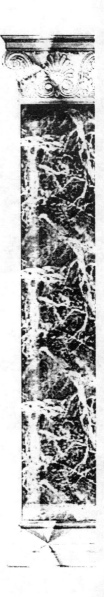

## YOU CAN NEVER HOPE TO ACHIEVE DIFFERENT RESULTS IF YOU OPERATE THE SAME WAY OVER AND OVER AGAIN.

*Luke 5:38  But new wine must be put into new bottles; and both are preserved.*

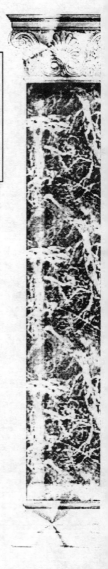

**SUCCESS KEY #66**

# THE CYCLE OF YOUR PRESENT WILL NEVER CHANGE UNTIL YOU CHANGE YOUR TACTICS.

*Luke 18:22-24 "Now when Jesus heard these things, he said unto him, Yet lackest thou one thing: sell all that thou hast, and distribute to the poor, and thou shalt have treasure in heaven: and come, follow Me. And when he heard this, he was very sorrowful, for he was very rich. And when Jesus saw that he was very sorrowful, he said, How hardly shall they that have riches enter into the kingdom of God!"*

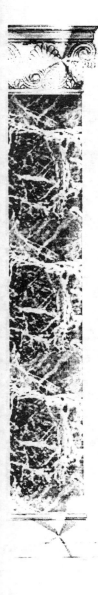

# WEALTH LOOKS FOR IDEAS, FOR THEY PROVIDE THE VACUUM FOR WEALTH TO FILL.

*Prov. 8:12  I wisdom dwell with prudence, and find out knowledge of witty inventions.*

**SUCCESS KEY #68**

# IF THERE ARE NO IDEAS, THERE CAN BE NO WEALTH.

*Ecclesiastes 7:12 "For wisdom is a defence, and money is a defence: but the excellency of knowledge is, that wisdom giveth life to them that have it."*

## WEALTH LOOKS FOR CREATORS, AND IS DRAWN TO THOSE WHO THINK LIKE GOD.

*Proverbs 8:12 "I wisdom dwell with prudence, and find out knowledge of witty inventions."*

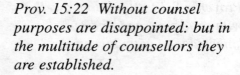

**SUCCESS KEY #70**

# WEALTH IS FOUND IN THE STRENGTH OF A PLAN.

*Prov. 15:22  Without counsel purposes are disappointed: but in the multitude of counsellors they are established.*

# PLANNING PROVIDES THE FRAME FOR AN IDEA TO GROW.

*Ps. 20:4 Grant thee according to thine own heart, and fulfil all thy counsel.*

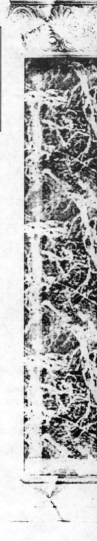

## SUCCESS KEY #72

# AN IDEA WITHOUT A PLAN CANNOT GO ANYWHERE.

*Proverbs 8:14 "Counsel is mine, and sound wisdom: I am understanding: I have strength."*

# WEALTH IS FOUND WITHIN ONE'S HANDS.

*Prov. 21:25 The desire of the slothful killeth him; for his hands refuse to labour.*

## SUCCESS KEY #74

### EVERY MAN IS EQUIPPED TO GENERATE WEALTH, BUT EVERY MAN IS NOT AWARE OF THE TOOLS HE POSSESSES.

*Proverbs 10:4 "He becometh poor that dealeth with a slack hand: but the hand of the diligent maketh rich."*

# GOD IS A GOD OF CHALLENGE....TAKE THE DARE!

*Mal. 3:10 "...prove me now herewith..."*

## SUCCESS KEY #76

**THE ONLY TIME THAT GOD INVITES MEN TO CHALLENGE HIM IS THROUGH THE PRACTICE OF TITHING...FOR IT IS AN INCORRUPTIBLE LAW THAT WILL EVOKE HIS FAVOR AND BLESSINGS.**

*Malachi 3:10 "Bring ye all the tithes into the storehouse, that there may be meat in mine house, and prove me now herewith, saith the Lord of hosts, if I will not open you the windows of heaven, and pour you out a blessing, that there shall not be room enough to receive it."*

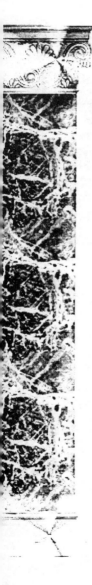

# MEN FAIL BECAUSE THEY FAIL TO ORGANIZE.

*Prov. 20:18  Every purpose is
established by counsel: and with
good advice make war.*

## ORGANIZATION IS A TYPE OF PLANNING, AND BRINGS ORDER—THE EVIDENCE OF GOD'S PRESENCE—ONTO THE SCENE.

*Psalms 49:10-11 "For he seeth that wise men die, likewise the fool and the brutish person perish, and leave their wealth to others. Their inward thought is, that their houses shall continue for ever, and their dwelling places to all generations; they call their lands after their own names."*

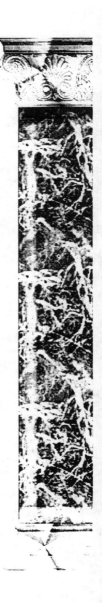

# MEN FAIL BECAUSE THEY BECOME PRIDEFUL.

*Prov. 29:23  A man's pride shall bring him low: but honour shall uphold the humble in spirit.*

## SUCCESS KEY #80

PRIDE EXALTS THE
CONFIDENCE THAT MAN
HAS IN HIMSELF AND
DENIES THE HONOR
THAT BELONGS TO GOD
AND GOD ALONE.

*Dan. 4:27 Wherefore, O king, let
my counsel be acceptable unto
thee, and break off thy sins by
righteousness, and thine iniquities
by showing mercy to the poor; if it
may be a lengthening of thy
tranquillity.*

# PRIDE PRECEDES THE MANIFESTATION OF A FALL BECAUSE IT HERALDS YOUR ASSUMPTION THAT YOU ARE WISER THAN GOD.

*Proverbs 16:18 "Pride goeth before destruction, and an haughty spirit before a fall."*

## SUCCESS KEY #82

# MEN FAIL BECAUSE THEY FEAR. FEAR WILL BLIND YOUR VISION AND ALTER YOUR PERCEPTION OF TRUTH.

*Proverbs 29:25 "The fear of a man bringeth a snare: but whoso putteth his trust in the Lord shall be safe."*

# MEN FAIL BECAUSE THEY REVEAL THEIR KNOWLEDGE.

*Prov. 17:28 Even a fool, when he holdeth his peace, is counted wise: and he that shutteth his lips is esteemed a man of understanding.*

Bishop E. Bernard Jordan

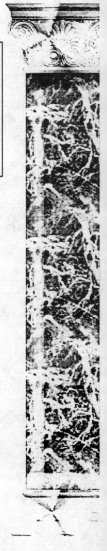

## SUCCESS KEY #84

# ONE SHOULD KNOW THE SEASON TO SPEAK AND THE SEASON TO REFRAIN.

*Proverbs 13:16 "Every prudent man dealeth with knowledge, but a fool layeth open his folly."*

# MEN FAIL BECAUSE THEY LOSE THEIR DREAM.

*Prov. 29:18  Where there is no vision, the people perish: but he that keepeth the law, happy is he.*

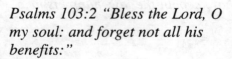

## SUCCESS KEY #86

# THE DREAM IS YOUR TARGET. WHEN IT IS LOST, YOU HAVE LOST YOUR DIRECTION.

*Psalms 103:2 "Bless the Lord, O my soul: and forget not all his benefits:"*

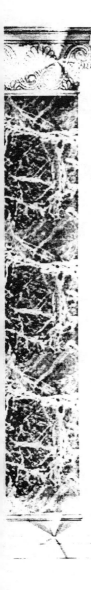

## SUCCESS KEY #87

# MEN FAIL BECAUSE THEY'RE DISLOYAL.

*Prov. 28:18 Whoso walketh uprightly shall be saved: but he that is perverse in his ways shall fall at once.*

## SUCCESS KEY #88

# DISLOYALTY CORRUPTS THE IMPARTATION OF YOUR MENTOR IN YOUR LIFE AND WILL SHORT-CIRCUIT THE CURRENTS OF SUCCESS IN YOUR LIFE!

*John 18:5 "They answered him, Jesus of Nazareth. Jesus saith unto them, I am he. And Judas also, which betrayed him, stood with them."*

# MEN FAIL WHEN THEY BECOME INDEPENDENT THINKERS.

*Prov. 28:26  He that trusteth in his own heart is a fool: but whoso walketh wisely, he shall be delivered.*

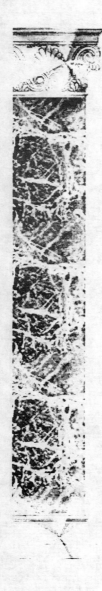

> ### SUCCESS KEY #90
>
> ## INDEPENDENCE IS A FORM OF PRIDE THAT ISOLATES YOU AND DENIES THE GREATNESS OF OTHERS.

*II Kings 5:20 "But Gehazi, the servant of Elisha the man of God, said, Behold, my master hath spared Namaan this Syrian, in not receiving at his hands that which he brought: but, as the Lord liveth, I will run after him, and take somewhat of him."*

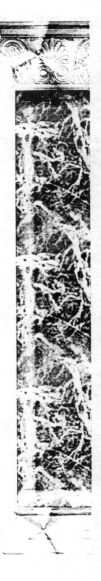

# MEN FAIL WHEN THEY ALLOW PROCRASTINATION TO STEAL THEIR TIME.

*Eccl. 3:1 To every thing there is a season, and a time to every purpose under the heaven:*

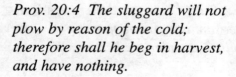

**SUCCESS KEY #92**

# PROCRASTINATION IS A SIGN OF GROSS DISRESPECT TO THE AUTHORITY OF TIME.

*Prov. 20:4  The sluggard will not plow by reason of the cold; therefore shall he beg in harvest, and have nothing.*

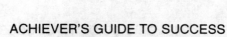

# WHEN REBELLION IS IN MANIFESTATION, REGARDLESS OF THE AREA, FAILURE WILL ANSWER.

*Proverbs 21:25 "The desire of the slothful killeth him; for his hands refuse to labour."*

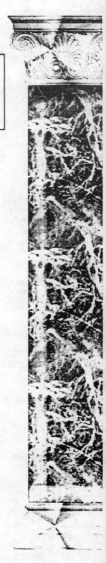

### SUCCESS KEY #94

## MEN FAIL WHEN THEY REJECT THE STRUGGLE.

*Prov. 19:20 Hear counsel, and receive instruction, that thou mayest be wise in thy latter end.*

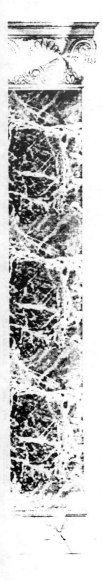
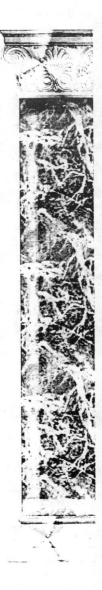

# STRUGGLE IS NECESSARY FOR DEVELOPMENT, FOR THE WAR OF OPPOSITION CREATES THE SPOILS OF STRENGTH.

*Luke 22:61 "And the Lord turned, and looked upon Peter. And Peter remembered the word of the Lord, how he had said unto him, Before the cock crow, thou shalt deny me thrice."*

**SUCCESS KEY #96**

# MEN FAIL WHEN THEY MAKE EXCUSES.

*Prov. 20:11  Even a child is known by his doings, whether his work be pure, and whether it be right.*

# EXCUSES ARE LIES THAT ARE CAREFULLY DISGUISED AS TRUTH.

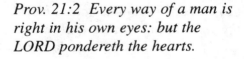

*Prov. 21:2 Every way of a man is right in his own eyes: but the LORD pondereth the hearts.*

## SUCCESS KEY #98

### EXCUSES HAVE THE ABILITY TO FOOL EVERYONE EXCEPT YOU AND GOD.

*Genesis 3:10 "And he said, I heard thy voice in the garden, and I was afraid, because I was naked; and I hid myself."*

# MEN FAIL WHEN THEY CAST BLAME.

*Gen. 3:12  And the man said, The woman whom thou gavest to be with me, she gave me of the tree, and I did eat.*

**SUCCESS KEY #100**

# BLAME IS THE REJECTION OF RESPONSIBILITY.

*Gen. 3:17 And unto Adam he said, Because thou hast hearkened unto the voice of thy wife, and hast eaten of the tree, of which I commanded thee, saying, Thou shalt not eat of it: cursed is the ground for thy sake; in sorrow shalt thou eat of it all the days of thy life;*

# RESPONSIBILITY IS THE ABILITY TO RESPOND.

*Prov. 7:2-3*
*Keep my commandments, and live;*
*and my law as the apple of thine*
*eye.*
*Bind them upon thy fingers, write*
*them upon the table of thine heart.*

## SUCCESS KEY #102

**UNLESS A MAN CAN DEVELOP HIS ABILITY TO RESPOND IN A GIVEN SITUATION, HE IS DOOMED TO FAIL, FOR HE HAS BECOME AN ICON WITHIN HIMSELF WHILE DENYING THE GRACE AND MERCY OF GOD.**

*Genesis 3:13 "And the Lord God said unto the woman, What is this that thou hast done? And the woman said, The serpent beguiled me, and I did eat."*

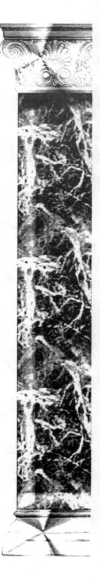

# MEN FAIL WHEN THEY LACK DISCIPLINE.

*Prov. 7:7*
*And beheld among the simple ones,*
*I discerned among the youths, a*
*young man void of understanding.*

*Prov. 7:22-23*
*He goeth after her straightway, as*
*an ox goeth to the slaughter, or as*
*a fool to the correction of the*
*stocks;*
*Till a dart strike through his liver;*
*as a bird hasteth to the snare, and*
*knoweth not that it is for his life.*

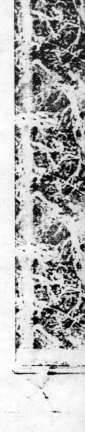

## SUCCESS KEY #104

# THE LACK OF DISCIPLINE DENOTES A LACK OF RESTRAINT. IF ONE CANNOT RULE HIS SPIRIT, HOW CAN HE TAKE A CITY?

*Proverbs 12:24 "The hand of the diligent shall bear rule: but the slothful shall be under tribute."*

# MEN FAIL WHEN THEY EXPECT UNRIGHTEOUS COMPENSATION.

*Prov. 17:23  A wicked man taketh a gift out of the bosom to pervert the ways of judgment.*

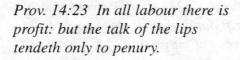

### SUCCESS KEY #106

# COMPENSATION CAN ONLY BE DEMANDED AS AN ACT OF RIGHTEOUSNESS.

*Prov. 14:23 In all labour there is profit: but the talk of the lips tendeth only to penury.*

# TO DEMAND COMPENSATION UNRIGHTEOUSLY IS TO ATTEMPT ILLEGAL ENTRANCE INTO PROSPERITY.

*Proverbs 13:4 "The soul of the sluggard desireth, and hath nothing: but the soul of the diligent shall be made fat."*

Bishop E. Bernard Jordan

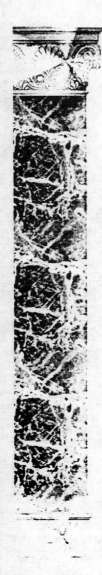

**SUCCESS KEY #108**

# MEN FAIL WHEN THEY CANNOT GIVE.

*Prov. 11:24 There is that scattereth, and yet increaseth; and there is that withholdeth more than is meet, but it tendeth to poverty.*

# A STINGY AND COVETOUS PERSON'S WEALTH WILL ROT.

*Prov. 11:29  He that troubleth his own house shall inherit the wind: and the fool shall be servant to the wise of heart.*

**SUCCESS KEY #110**

# WHEN MONEY IS NOT ALLOWED TO FLOW, THE LAWS OF ITS LIFE ARE VIOLATED.

*Proverbs 1:17-19 "Surely in vain the net is spread in the sight of any bird. And they lay in wait for their own blood; they lurk privily for their own lives. So are the ways of every one that is greedy of gain; which taketh away the life of the owners thereof."*

# MEN FAIL WHEN THEY REJECT GOD.

*Ps. 14:1 To the chief Musician, A Psalm of David. The fool hath said in his heart, There is no God. They are corrupt, they have done abominable works, there is none that doeth good.*

**SUCCESS KEY #112**

## TO REJECT GOD IS TO REJECT THE SOURCE OF ALL THINGS.

*Gen. 1:1 In the beginning God created the heaven and the earth.*

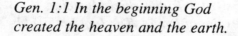

# IF YOU REJECT THE SOURCE, YOU CANNOT ATTAIN.

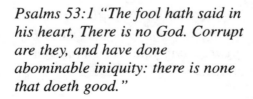

*Psalms 53:1 "The fool hath said in his heart, There is no God. Corrupt are they, and have done abominable iniquity: there is none that doeth good."*

## SUCCESS KEY #114

# MEN FAIL WHEN THEY CANNOT SERVE.

*Matt. 20:26  But it shall not be so among you: but whosoever will be great among you, let him be your minister;*

# TO REFUSE SERVITUDE IS TO ATTEMPT ILLEGAL RULE, FOR PROMOTION COMES FROM GOD.

*II Kings 4:31 "And Gehazi passed on before them, and laid the staff upon the face of the child; but there was neither voice, nor hearing. Wherefore he went again to meet him, and told him, saying, The child is not awaked."*

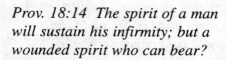

# EMOTIONS ARE NOT TO BE SUPPRESSED, BUT MANAGED.

*Prov. 18:14 The spirit of a man will sustain his infirmity; but a wounded spirit who can bear?*

# IF EMOTIONS ARE NOT MANAGED, THEY CAN DISTORT YOUR PERCEPTION OF TRUTH.

*Proverbs 16:32 "He that is slow to anger is better than the mighty; and he that ruleth his spirit than he that taketh a city."*

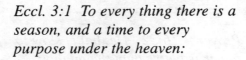

## SUCCESS KEY #118

# MEN FAIL WHEN THEY CANNOT SEE PURPOSE.

*Eccl. 3:1  To every thing there is a season, and a time to every purpose under the heaven:*

# WHEN PURPOSE IS NOT DISCERNED, DESTINATION IS OVERTURNED.

*I Samuel 15:24 "And Saul said unto Samuel, I have sinned: for I have transgressed the commandment of the Lord, and thy words: because I feared the people, and obeyed their voice."*

Bishop E. Bernard Jordan

**SUCCESS KEY #120**

# MEN FAIL WHEN THEY REJECT AUTHORITY.

*Prov. 19:16  He that keepeth the commandment keepeth his own soul; but he that despiseth his ways shall die.*

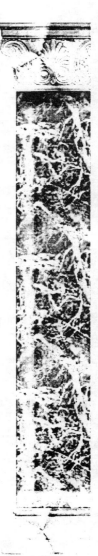

# THE REJECTION OF AUTHORITY IS THE EMBRACE OF DEFILEMENT.

*Prov. 19:25-26 Smite a scorner, and the simple will beware: and reprove one that hath understanding, and he will understand knowledge.*
*He that wasteth his father, and chaseth away his mother, is a son that causeth shame, and bringeth reproach.*

**SUCCESS KEY #122**

## AUTHORITY PROVIDES A COVERING; THE REJECTION OF IT BRINGS AN EXPOSURE TO THE ELEMENTS OF FAILURE.

*Proverbs 17:11 "An evil man seeketh only rebellion: therefore a cruel messenger shall be sent against him."*

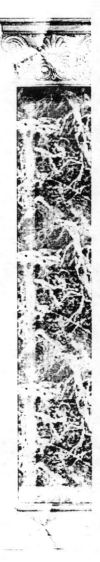

## MEN FAIL WHEN THEY EMBRACE A LIE.

*Gen. 3:23 Therefore the LORD God sent him forth from the garden of Eden, to till the ground from whence he was taken.*

## SUCCESS KEY #124

# A LIE WILL LEAD YOU TO DESTRUCTION AND VEIL ITSELF AS A WORKABLE GOAL.

*Proverbs 19:5 "A false witness shall not be unpunished, and he that speaketh lies shall not escape."*

# MEN FAIL WHEN THEY MISS THEIR MOMENT.

*Matt. 25:10 And while they went to buy, the bridegroom came; and they that were ready went in with him to the marriage: and the door was shut.*

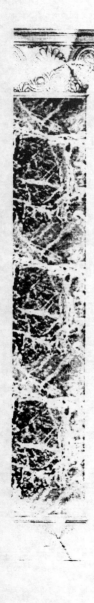

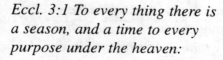

**SUCCESS KEY #126**

# IF YOU TRY TO PLANT TOMATOES IN THE WINTER, THEY WILL DIE.

*Eccl. 3:1 To every thing there is a season, and a time to every purpose under the heaven:*

# FAILURE WILL APPEAR WHEN YOU CANNOT ASCERTAIN YOUR TIME.

*Ecclesiastes 3:1 "To every thing there is a season, and a time to every purpose under the heaven:"*

## SUCCESS KEY #128

# MEN FAIL WHEN THEY MISS THEIR CONNECTIONS.

*1 Sam. 10:9 -10 And it was so, that when he had turned his back to go from Samuel, God gave him another heart: and all those signs came to pass that day.*
*And when they came thither to the hill, behold, a company of prophets met him; and the spirit of God came upon him, and he*
*prophesied among them.*

**OBEDIENCE TO THE
INSTRUCTIONS OF THE
LORD WILL CAUSE
YOU TO RECEIVE HIS
SUPPLY THROUGH
THE VESSELS OF HIS
COMMANDMENT.**

*1 Kin. 17:15-16 And she went and
did according to the saying of
Elijah: and she, and he, and her
house, did eat many days.
And the barrel of meal wasted not,
neither did the cruse of oil fail,
according to the word of the
LORD, which he spake by Elijah.*

## SUCCESS KEY #130

# WHEN YOU MOVE IN DISOBEDIENCE, YOU MAY MISS YOUR SUPPLY.

*I Kings 17:9 "Arise, get thee to Zarephath, which belongeth to Zidon, and dwell there: behold, I have commanded a widow woman there to sustain thee."*

# MEN FAIL WHEN THEY MISS THEIR LOCATION.

*Num. 14:22-23  Because all those men which have seen my glory, and my miracles, which I did in Egypt and in the wilderness, and have tempted me now these ten times, and have not hearkened to my voice;*
*Surely they shall not see the land which I sware unto their fathers, neither shall any of them that provoked me see it:*

## SUCCESS KEY #132

# IT IS IMPORTANT TO KNOW THE PLACE OF YOUR ASSIGNMENT.

*2 Kin. 2:2 And Elijah said unto Elisha, Tarry here, I pray thee; for the LORD hath sent me to Bethel. And Elisha said unto him, As the LORD liveth, and as thy soul liveth, I will not leave thee. So they went down to Bethel.*

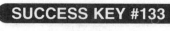
## SUCCESS KEY #133

# WHEN YOU ARE NOT IN THE PLACE OF YOUR PROVISION, YOU CANNOT RECEIVE.

*I Kings 17:3-4 "Get thee hence, and turn thee eastward, and hide thyself by the brook Cherith, that is before Jordan. And it shall be, that thou shalt drink of the brook; and I have commanded the ravens to feed thee there."*

### SUCCESS KEY #134

# MEN FAIL WHEN THEY CANNOT FOLLOW DIRECTIONS.

*I Kings 13:21-22  "And he cried unto the man of God that came from Judah, saying, Thus saith the Lord, Forasmuch as thou hast disobeyed the mouth of the Lord, and hast not kept the commandment which the Lord thy God commanded thee, But camest back, and hast eaten bread and drunk water in the place, of the which the Lord did say to thee, Eat no bread, and drink no water; thy carcase shall not come unto the sepulchre of thy fathers."*

# MEN FAIL WHEN THEY CANNOT SEE THEIR WORTH.

*Prov. 3:5 ᛫ Trust in the LORD with all thine heart; and lean not unto thine own understanding.*

## SUCCESS KEY #136

# IGNORANCE OF YOUR POTENTIAL WILL CAUSE YOU TO UNDERESTIMATE THE ABILITY OF GOD WITHIN YOU.

*Judg. 6:15 And he said unto him, Oh my Lord, wherewith shall I save Israel? behold, my family is poor in Manasseh, and I am the least in my father's house.*

# IF YOU ARE DEAF TO THE VOICE OF INSTRUCTION, YOU WILL NOT HEAR YOUR MIRACLE CALL YOUR NAME.

*II Kings 6:15-18 "And when the servant of the man of God was risen early, and gone forth, behold, an host compassed the city both with horses and chariots. And his servant said unto him, Alas, my master! how shall we do? And he answered, Fear not: for they that be with us are more than they that be with them. And Elisha prayed, and said, Lord, I pray thee, open his eyes that he may see. And the Lord opened the eyes, of the young man; and he saw: and, behold, the mountains were full of horses and chariots of fire round about Elisha."*

## SUCCESS KEY #138

# MEN FAIL WHEN THEY DISRESPECT OTHERS.

*Mal. 2:9 Therefore have I also made you contemptible and base before all the people, according as ye have not kept my ways, but have been partial in the law.*

# ONE CAN NEVER PROSPER UPON THE DENIGRATION OF ANOTHER.

*Job 13:10  He will surely reprove you, if ye do secretly accept persons.*

Bishop E. Bernard Jordan

# LOVE IS THE HIGHEST LAW OF THE UNIVERSE.

*II Samuel 21:7 "But the king spared Mephibosheth, the son of Jonathan the son of Saul, because of the Lord's oath that was between them, between David and Jonathan the son of Saul."*

# MEN FAIL WHEN THEY ENVY ANOTHER.

*Prov. 14:30 A sound heart is the life of the flesh: but envy the rottenness of the bones.*

## SUCCESS KEY #142

**ENVY STRIPS YOU OF THE AWARENESS OF YOUR PERSONAL POTENTIAL, THEREBY SENTENCING YOU TO A MORASS OF FRUSTRATION AS YOU ARE CRIPPLED THROUGH THE POWER OF COMPETITION.**

*Gen. 4:5-8  But unto Cain and to his offering he had not respect. And Cain was very wroth, and his countenance fell. And the LORD said unto Cain, Why art thou wroth? and why is thy countenance fallen?*
*If thou doest well, shalt thou not be accepted? and if thou doest not well, sin lieth at the door. And unto thee shall be his desire, and thou shalt rule over him. And Cain talked with Abel his brother: and it came to pass, when they were in the field, that Cain rose up against Abel his brother, and slew him.*

# WEALTH RESPONDS TO THE DOMINATING THOUGHT IN YOUR MIND.

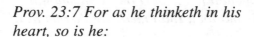

*Prov. 23:7 For as he thinketh in his heart, so is he:*

## SUCCESS KEY #144

### YOU WILL ATTRACT WHAT YOU TRULY BELIEVE, FOR YOUR DOMINATING THOUGHT WILL FORCE ITS EXPRESSION IN YOUR LIFE.

*Joshua 1:8 "This book of the law shall not depart out of thy mouth; but thou shalt meditate therein day and night, that thou mayest observe to do according to all that is written therein: for then thou shalt make thy way prosperous, and then thou shalt have good success."*

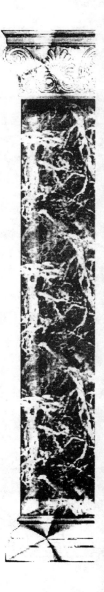

# Wealth begins in your head.

*Rom. 12:2  And be not conformed to this world: but be ye transformed by the renewing of your mind, that ye may prove what is that good, and acceptable, and perfect, will of God.*

**SUCCESS KEY #146**

YOUR MIND REALLY
MATTERS, WHICH IS
WHY YOUR MIND MUST
BE RENEWED THROUGH
THE WORD OF GOD.

*Ephesians 4:23 "And be renewed
in the spirit of your mind;"*

# DESIRE IS A SIGNAL THAT GOD IS IN YOUR DREAM.

*Psalms 145:19 "He will fulfill the desire of them that fear him:"*

**SUCCESS KEY #148**

## "DESIRE" LITERALLY MEANS "OF THE FATHER."

*1 John 5:14-15*
*And this is the confidence that we have in him, that, if we ask any thing according to his will, he heareth us:*
*And if we know that he hear us, whatsoever we ask, we know that we have the petitions that we desired of him.*

# YOUR DESIRE BECOMES THE EVIDENCE THAT GOD HAS CALLED YOU TO MANIFEST HIS VISION.

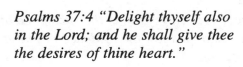

*Psalms 37:4 "Delight thyself also in the Lord; and he shall give thee the desires of thine heart."*

Bishop E. Bernard Jordan

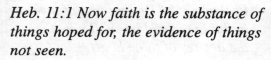

## SUCCESS KEY #150

# IF YOU CAN SEE TO AIM, YOU CAN HIT YOUR TARGET.

*Heb. 11:1 Now faith is the substance of things hoped for, the evidence of things not seen.*

# BLINDNESS PREVENTS ACCURACY IN YOUR STEERING.

*Is. 6:10 Make the heart of this people fat, and make their ears heavy, and shut their eyes; lest they see with their eyes, and hear with their ears, and understand with their heart, and convert, and be healed.*

Bishop E. Bernard Jordan

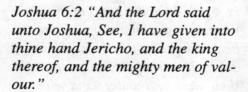

### SUCCESS KEY #152

# IF YOU DON'T KNOW WHAT YOU'RE LOOKING AT, YOU MAY HIT A WALL.

*Joshua 6:2 "And the Lord said unto Joshua, See, I have given into thine hand Jericho, and the king thereof, and the mighty men of valour."*

**152** ACHIEVER'S GUIDE TO SUCCESS

# TRUTH IS THE FOUNDATION FOR TRUE RICHES.

*Proverbs 10:22 "The blessing of the Lord, it maketh rich, and he addeth no sorrow with it."*

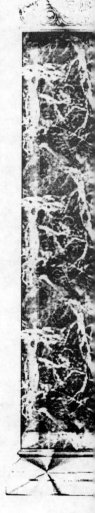

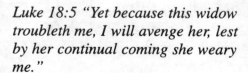

SUCCESS KEY #154

# TENACITY WILL ENABLE YOU TO KEEP ON FIGHTING WITH PERSISTENCE UNTIL YOU WIN THE SPOILS.

*Luke 18:5 "Yet because this widow troubleth me, I will avenge her, lest by her continual coming she weary me."*

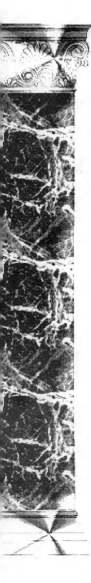

# DETERMINATION BRINGS COMPENSATION.

*Prov. 8:17-18*
*I love them that love me; and those*
*that seek me early shall find me.*
*Riches and honour are with me;*
*yea, durable riches and righteous-*
*ness.*

SUCCESS KEY #156

# AN ATTITUDE THAT WILL NOT LOSE FOCUS WILL ENCOMPASS THE POWER OF FAITH AND FORCE THE MANIFESTATION OF THE DREAM.

*Proverbs 10:4 "He becometh poor that dealeth with a slack hand: but the hand of the diligent maketh rich."*

## ALL DREAMS NEED A DEADLINE, BECAUSE A DEADLINE CREATES THE FRAME FOR ITS CONSTRUCTION.

*Psalms 69:13 "But as for me, my prayer is unto thee, O Lord, in an acceptable time: O God, in the multitude of thy mercy hear me, in the truth of thy salvation."*

# CULTIVATE IMAGINATION...IT'S THE PLACE OF YOUR IDEAS.

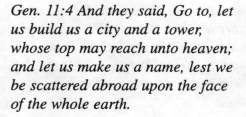

*Gen. 11:4 And they said, Go to, let us build us a city and a tower, whose top may reach unto heaven; and let us make us a name, lest we be scattered abroad upon the face of the whole earth.*

# IMAGINATION IS THE ABILITY TO SEE UNHARNESSED POSSIBILITIES.

*Genesis 11:6 "And the Lord said, Behold, the people is one, and they have all one language; and this they begin to do: and now nothing will be restrained from them, which they have imagined to do."*

Bishop E. Bernard Jordan

## SUCCESS KEY #160

# IMAGINATION SEEKS CREATION.

*Genesis 11:4 "And they said, Go to, let us build us a city and a tower, whose top may reach unto heaven; and let us make us a name, lest we be scattered abroad upon the face of the whole earth."*

# THE SLOTHFUL PERSON IS THE HABITATION OF POVERTY, FOR THEY DO NOT OPERATE BY THE LAWS OF PROCUREMENT.

*Proverbs 24:33-34 "Yet a little sleep, yet a little slumber, a little folding of the hands to sleep: So shall thy poverty come as one that travelleth; and thy want as an armed man."*

### SUCCESS KEY #162

## MONEY SEEKS THE MINDS THAT ARE READY.

*Proverbs 24:14 "So shall the knowledge of wisdom be unto thy soul: when thou hast found it, then there shall be a reward, and thy expectation shall not be cut off."*

# YOUR ECONOMICS ARE LEFT UP TO YOU!

*Luke 19:15 And it came to pass, that when he was returned, having received the kingdom, then he commanded these servants to be called unto him, to whom he had given the money, that he might know how much every man had gained by trading.*

## SUCCESS KEY #164

# DESTINY IS NOT LEFT UP TO CHANCE BUT IT IS A MATTER OF CHOICE!

*Deuteronomy 30:19 "I call heaven and earth to record this day against you, that I have set before you life and death, blessing and cursing: therefore choose life, that both thou and thy seed may live:"*

# LEARN TO SEE
# IN THE DARK.

*1 Cor. 2:9-10*
*But as it is written, Eye hath not seen, nor ear heard, neither have entered into the heart of man, the things which God hath prepared for them that love him.*
*But God hath revealed them unto us by his Spirit: for the Spirit searcheth all things, yea, the deep things of God.*

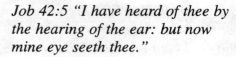

**SUCCESS KEY #166**

# ONE MUST ALWAYS LOOK BEYOND HIS PRESENT IN ORDER TO SEE HIS FUTURE.

*Job 42:5 "I have heard of thee by the hearing of the ear: but now mine eye seeth thee."*

# START GROPING WHILE YOU'RE HOPING!

*James 2:20 But wilt thou know, O vain man, that faith without works is dead?*

## SUCCESS KEY #168

### SOMETIMES, YOU MAY NOT SEE THE WHOLE PICTURE, BUT DON'T BE AFRAID TO REACH TOWARDS THE PART YOU CAN SEE!

*Exodus 14:10 & 13 "And when Pharaoh drew nigh, the children of Israel lifted up their eyes, and, behold, the Egyptians marched after them; and they were sore afraid: and the children of Israel cried out unto the Lord.*
*And Moses said unto the people, Fear ye not, stand still, and see the salvation of the Lord, which he will shew to you to day: for the Egyptians whom ye have seen to day, ye shall see them again no more for ever."*

# POVERTY AND RICHES BOTH SEEK HABITATION...THEY WILL RESPOND TO YOUR MISEDUCATION.

*Is. 48:17 Thus saith the LORD, thy Redeemer, the Holy One of Israel; I am the LORD thy God which teacheth thee to profit, which leadeth thee by the way that thou shouldest go.*

## SUCCESS KEY #170

# POVERTY WILL MANIFEST IN THE VACUUM OF WISDOM.

*Proverbs 1:7 "The fear of the Lord is the beginning of knowledge: but fools despise wisdom and instruction."*

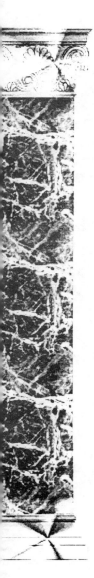

# "YES" HIDES IN THE SKIRTS OF A "NO".

*Luke 18:4-5  And he would not for a while: but afterward he said within himself, Though I fear not God, nor regard man;*
*Yet because this widow troubleth me, I will avenge her, lest by her continual coming she weary me.*

SUCCESS KEY #172

## THE FIRST ANSWER IS NOT ALWAYS THE FINAL ANSWER.

*Luke 11:7-8 And he from within shall answer and say, Trouble me not: the door is now shut, and my children are with me in bed; I cannot rise and give thee.*
*I say unto you, Though he will not rise and give him, because he is his friend, yet because of his importunity he will rise and give him as many as he needeth.*

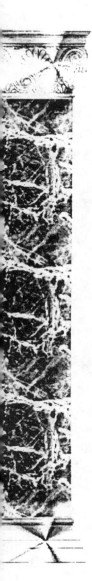

# TIME MUST BE GRANTED TO INVOKE THE POWER OF PERSUASION IN A MATTER.

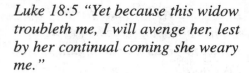

*Luke 18:5 "Yet because this widow troubleth me, I will avenge her, lest by her continual coming she weary me."*

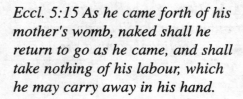

**SUCCESS KEY #174**

# DEFEAT TEASES THE ELITE.

*Eccl. 5:15 As he came forth of his mother's womb, naked shall he return to go as he came, and shall take nothing of his labour, which he may carry away in his hand.*

# THOSE WHO HAVE MASTERED THE LAWS OF ACQUISITION ARE NOT MOVED BY THE APPEARANCE OF SETBACKS.

*Rom. 4:20 He staggered not at the promise of God through unbelief; but was strong in faith, giving glory to God;*

**SUCCESS KEY #176**

## FAILURE IS SIMPLY A SIGNAL TO TRY IT AGAIN.

*Ecclesiastes 9:11 "I returned, and saw under the sun, that the race is not to the swift, nor the battle to the strong, neither yet bread to the wise, nor yet riches to men of understanding, nor yet favour to men of skill; but time and chance happeneth to them all."*

# THE NATURAL ORDER OF LIFE IS TO GIVE AND TO GET.

*Luke 6:38 "Give, and it shall be given unto you; good measure, pressed down, and shaken together, and running over, shall men give into your bosom. For with the same measure that ye mete withal shall it be measured to you again."*

Bishop E. Bernard Jordan

### SUCCESS KEY #178

## WEALTH CAN ONLY BE PRODUCED BY A VISIONARY—SOMEONE WHO HAS GIVEN HIMSELF TO LEARNING DISCIPLINE.

*Proverbs 1:5-6 "A wise man will hear, and will increase learning; and a man of understanding shall attain unto wise counsels:*
*To understand a proverb, and the interpretation; the words of the wise, and their dark sayings."*

# JOSHUA IS NOT AFRAID OF A CHALLENGE.

*Num. 14:9 Only rebel not ye against the LORD, neither fear ye the people of the land; for they are bread for us: their defence is departed from them, and the LORD is with us: fear them not.*

## SUCCESS KEY #180

## JOSHUA UNDERSTANDS THAT CHALLENGE IS THE PROCESS OF GROWTH WITH TREASURES THAT MAY BE OBTAINED AT EACH STAGE.

*Numbers 14:6-9 "And Joshua the son of Nun, and Caleb the son of Jephunneh, which were of them that searched the land, rent their clothes: And they spake unto all the company of the children of Israel, saying, The land, which we passed through to search it, is an exceeding good land.*
*If the Lord delight in us, then he will bring us into this land, and give it us; a land which floweth with milk and honey. Only rebel not ye against the Lord, neither fear ye the people of the land; for they are bread for us: their defence is departed from them, and the Lord is with us: fear them not."*

# JOSHUA IS A DISCIPLINED MAN.

*Josh. 11:15*
*As the LORD commanded Moses*
*his servant, so did Moses command*
*Joshua, and so did Joshua; he left*
*nothing undone of all that the*
*LORD commanded Moses.*

**SUCCESS KEY #182**

# JOSHUA UNDERSTANDS THAT HE MUST FOLLOW BEFORE HE CAN LEAD.

*Ex. 24:13 And Moses rose up, and his minister Joshua: and Moses went up into the mount of God.*

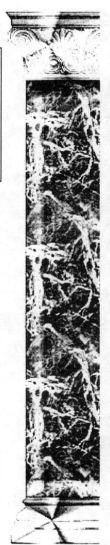

# JOSHUA KNOWS HOW TO TAME HIS APPETITES AND RULE HIS SPIRIT.

*Numbers 27:18-20 "And the Lord said unto Moses, Take thee Joshua the son of Nun, a man in whom is the spirit, and lay thine hand upon him: And set him before Eleazar the priest, and before all the congregation; and give him a charge in their sight. And thou shalt put some of thine honour upon him that all the congregation of the children of Israel may be obedient."*

**SUCCESS KEY #184**

## JOSHUA THINKS WITH A RENEWED MIND.

*Deut. 34:9 And Joshua the son of Nun was full of the spirit of wisdom; for Moses had laid his hands upon him: and the children of Israel hearkened unto him, and did as the LORD commanded Moses.*

# JOSHUA IS A MAN OF PRINCIPLE AND UNDERSTANDING.

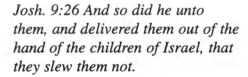

*Josh. 9:26 And so did he unto them, and delivered them out of the hand of the children of Israel, that they slew them not.*

Bishop E. Bernard Jordan

## SUCCESS KEY #186

# JOSHUA IS A MAN WHO COMPREHENDS THE ABILITY OF GOD WITHIN.

*Deuteronomy 1:38 "But Joshua the son of Nun, which standeth before thee, he shall go in thither: encourage him: for he shall cause Israel to inherit it."*

**186** ACHIEVER'S GUIDE TO SUCCESS

# JOSHUA SEEKS THE HARD PROBLEMS.

*Josh. 7:19 And Joshua said unto Achan, My son, give, I pray thee, glory to the LORD God of Israel, and make confession unto him; and tell me now what thou hast done; hide it not from me.*

## SUCCESS KEY #188

JOSHUA IS NOT AFRAID
OF A STRUGGLE, FOR
HE UNDERSTANDS THAT
VICTORY ONLY APPEARS
FOR A PRICE.

*Joshua 3:10*
*"And Joshua said, Hereby ye shall*
*know that the living God is among*
*you, and that he will without fail*
*drive out from before you the*
*Canbaanites, and the Hittites, and*
*the Hivites, and the Perizites, and*
*the Girgashites, and the Amorites,*
*and the Jebusites."*

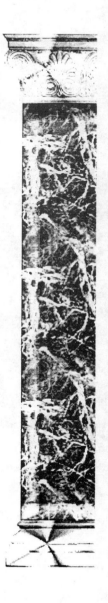

# JOSHUA IS STRONG AND OF A GOOD COURAGE.

*Josh. 10:40 So Joshua smote all the country of the hills, and of the south, and of the vale, and of the springs, and all their kings: he left none remaining, but utterly destroyed all that breathed, as the LORD God of Israel commanded.*

**SUCCESS KEY #190**

**JOSHUA DERIVES HIS STRENGTH FROM HIS KNOWLEDGE OF THE STRENGTH OF GOD, AND REMAINS FEARLESS FOR GOD IS WITH HIM.**

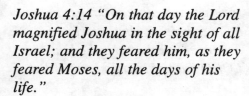

*Joshua 4:14 "On that day the Lord magnified Joshua in the sight of all Israel; and they feared him, as they feared Moses, all the days of his life."*

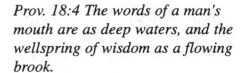

## SUCCESS KEY #191

# JOSHUA SPEAKS THE RIGHT THINGS TO HIMSELF.

*Prov. 18:4 The words of a man's mouth are as deep waters, and the wellspring of wisdom as a flowing brook.*

## SUCCESS KEY #192

# JOSHUA'S INNER CONVERSATIONS REFLECT HIS MEDITATION UPON THE WORD OF GOD.

Joshua 1:8 *"This book of the law shall not depart out of thy mouth; but thou shalt meditate therein day and night, that thou mayest observe to do according to all that is written therein: for then thou shalt make thy way prosperous, and then thou shalt have good success."*

# JOSHUA DISCERNS THE SEASONS AND THE TIMES.

*Josh. 18:2-3 And there remained among the children of Israel seven tribes, which had not yet received their inheritance.*
*And Joshua said unto the children of Israel, How long are ye slack to go to possess the land, which the LORD God of your fathers hath given you?*

**SUCCESS KEY #194**

## JOSHUA KNOWS WHEN TO PLANT AND REAP, AND WILL UTILIZE EACH SEASON (TO HIS ADVANTAGE.)

*Joshua 14:10 "And now, behold, the Lord hath kept me alive, as he said, these forty and five years, even since the Lord spake this word unto Moses, while the children of Israel wandered in the wilderness: and now, lo, I am this day fourscore and five years old. As yet I am as strong this day as I was in the day that Moses sent me: as my strength was then, even so is my strength now, for war, both to go out, and to come in."*

# JOSHUA EMBRACES CHANGE AS THE CATALYST TO NEW PLATEAUS IN LIFE.

*Josh. 5:2-3  At that time the LORD said unto Joshua, Make thee sharp knives, and circumcise again the children of Israel the second time. And Joshua made him sharp knives, and circumcised the children of Israel at the hill of the foreskins.*

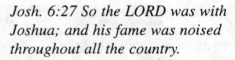

## SUCCESS KEY #196

JOSHUA IS NOT A MAN OF STAGNATION, BUT HE IS A MAN OF GREATNESS THAT CONTINUALLY SEEKS TO LOOK OVER NEW HORIZONS.

*Josh. 6:27 So the LORD was with Joshua; and his fame was noised throughout all the country.*

# JOSHUA IS A MAN WHO KNOWS HIS GOD AND WILL NOT ENTERTAIN ANY PRESENCE WHICH ALTERS HIS FAITH IN GOD.

*Joshua 11:20 "For it was of the Lord to harden their hearts, that they should come against Israel in battle, that he might destroy them utterly, and that they might have no favour, but he might destroy them, as the Lord commanded Moses."*

Bishop E. Bernard Jordan

## SUCCESS KEY #198

# JOSHUA WILL ATTACK THE GATES OF HELL.

*Deut. 1:38 But Joshua the son of Nun, which standeth before thee, he shall go in thither: encourage him: for he shall cause Israel to inherit it.*

## JOSHUA IS A MAN OF GREAT EXPLOITS WHO IS NEVER INTIMIDATED BY THE PRESENCE OF HELL.

*Joshua 10:42 "And all these kings and their land did Joshua take at one time, because the Lord God fought for Israel."*

**SUCCESS KEY #200**

## JOSHUA UNDERSTANDS THE ART OF WAR AND UNDERSTANDS THAT HELL MUST BE DRIVEN OFF THE LAND.

*Joshua 10:40 "So Joshua smote all the country of the hills, and of the south, and of the vale, and of the springs, and all their kings: he left none remaining, but utterly destroyed all that breathed, as the Lord God of Israel commanded."*

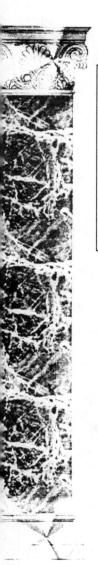

## JOSHUA DOESN'T SLEEP WITH THE ENEMY, FOR HE KNOWS THAT COMPROMISE WILL CORRUPT HIS VISION.

*Num. 32:12 Save Caleb the son of Jephunneh the Kenezite, and Joshua the son of Nun: for they have wholly followed the LORD.*

## SUCCESS KEY #202

# JOSHUA LOOKS PAST CONFUSION TO DISCERN VISITATION.

*Josh. 7:25-26 And Joshua said, Why hast thou troubled us? the LORD shall trouble thee this day. And all Israel stoned him with stones, and burned them with fire, after they had stoned them with stones.*

*And they raised over him a great heap of stones unto this day. So the LORD turned from the fierceness of his anger. Wherefore the name of that place was called, The valley of Achor, unto this day.*

# JOSHUA UNDERSTANDS THAT ALL THINGS WORK TOGETHER FOR GOOD TO THEM THAT LOVE GOD AND WHO ARE THE CALLED ACCORDING TO HIS PURPOSE.

*Joshua 7:6-7 "And Joshua rent his clothes, and fell to the earth upon his face before the ark of the Lord until the eventide, he and the elders of Israel, and put dust upon their heads. And Joshua said, Alas, O Lord God, wherefore hast thou at all brought this people over Jordan, to deliver us into the hand of the Amorites, to destroy us? would to God we had been content, and dwelt on the other side Jordan!"*

## SUCCESS KEY #204

### JOSHUA UNDERSTANDS ORDER AS THE EVIDENCE OF GOD IN OPERATION, FOR GOD IS A GOD OF ORDER.

*Joshua 6:10 "And Joshua had commanded the people, saying, Ye shall not shout, nor make any noise with your voice, neither shall any word proceed out of your mouth, until the day I bid you shout; then shall ye shout."*

# JOSHUA WILL REST TO REGAIN STRENGTH, BUT HE'S NEVER LAZY.

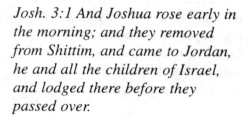

*Josh. 3:1 And Joshua rose early in the morning; and they removed from Shittim, and came to Jordan, he and all the children of Israel, and lodged there before they passed over.*

Bishop E. Bernard Jordan

## SUCCESS KEY #206

# LAZINESS IS A STATE OF INACTIVITY WITHOUT PURPOSE.

*Joshua 1:14b-15 "...ye shall pass before your brethren armed, all the mighty men of valour, and help them; Until the Lord hath given your brethren rest, as he hast given you, and they also possessed the land which the Lord your God giveth them: then ye shall return until the land of your possession, and enjoy it, which Moses the Lord's servant gave you on this side Jordan toward the sunrising."*

# JOSHUA FOLLOWS INSTRUCTIONS AND HAS AN EAR TO HEAR WHAT THE SPIRIT OF THE LORD IS SAYING.

Joshua 8:26 *"For Joshua drew not his hand back wherewith he stretched out the spear, until he had utterly destroyed all the inhabitants of Ai. Only the cattle and the spoil of that city Israel took for a prey unto themselves, according unto the word of the Lord which he commanded Joshua."*

## SUCCESS KEY #208

# JOSHUA ECHOES
# HIS MENTOR.

*Josh. 1:12-13 And to the Reubenites,
and to the Gadites, and to half the
tribe of Manasseh, spake Joshua,
saying,
Remember the word which Moses the
servant of the LORD commanded
you, saying, The LORD your God
hath given you rest, and hath given
you this land.*

# JOSHUA DOES NOT ENTERTAIN HIS OWN VISION UNTIL THE DEATH OF HIS MENTOR.

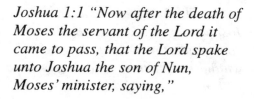

*Joshua 1:1 "Now after the death of Moses the servant of the Lord it came to pass, that the Lord spake unto Joshua the son of Nun, Moses' minister, saying,"*

**SUCCESS KEY #210**

## JOSHUA'S MANHOOD IS TRANSFERABLE.

*Josh. 1:16 And they answered Joshua, saying, All that thou commandest us we will do, and whithersoever thou sendest us, we will go.*

# JOSHUA'S EXAMPLE OF LIFE WAS DUPLICATED AMONGST THE MEN OF ISRAEL, FOR THEY WERE ABLE TO FOLLOW SURE FOOTSTEPS TO SUCCESS.

*Joshua 1:16 "And they answered Joshua, saying, All that thou commandest us we will do, and whithersoever thou sendest us, we will go. According as we hearkened unto Moses in all things, so will we hearken unto thee: only the Lord thy God be with thee, as he was with Moses."*

## SUCCESS KEY #212

### JOSHUA KNOWS REBELLION IS AS THE SIN OF WITCHCRAFT... IT ATTEMPTS TO CURSE WHAT GOD HAS BLESSED.

*Joshua 11:15 "As the Lord commanded Moses his servant, so did Moses command Joshua, and so did Joshua; he left nothing undone of all that the Lord commanded Moses."*

# JOSHUA MASTERS HIS INTERNAL ENEMIES.

*Joshua 8:35 "There was not a word of all that Moses command-ed, which Joshua read not before all the congregation of Israel, with the women, and the little ones, and the strangers that were conversant among them."*

**SUCCESS KEY #214**

# JOSHUA HAS ENCOUNTERED THE TRUTH ABOUT HIMSELF, AND PURSUES DOMINION OVER FOLLY WITHIN.

*Josh. 6:10 And Joshua had commanded the people, saying, Ye shall not shout, nor make any noise with your voice, neither shall any word proceed out of your mouth, until the day I bid you shout; then shall ye shout.*

## SUCCESS KEY #215

# JOSHUA IS NOT MOVED BY THE EXPECTATIONS OF OTHERS.

*Joshua 8:9  "Joshua therefore sent them forth: and they went to lie in ambush, and abode between Bethel and Ai, on the west side of Ai: but Joshua lodged that night among the people."*

Bishop E. Bernard Jordan

## SUCCESS KEY #216

# JOSHUA IS LIBERATED FROM BEING A "PEOPLE-PLEASER," FOR HE UNDERSTANDS THAT THE APPROVAL OF MEN IS ALWAYS DECEPTIVE AND ELUSIVE, AND GOD IS THE ONLY SOURCE OF APPROVAL.

*Joshua 11:23 "So Joshua took the whole land, according to all that the Lord said unto Moses; and Joshua gave it for an inheritance unto Israel according to their divisions by their tribes. And the land rested from war."*

# JOSHUA IS AN ACHIEVER.
# JOSHUA WAS ABLE TO EXECUTE THE NEXT PHASE OF HIS MENTOR'S MINISTRY UPON THE DEATH OF MOSES.

*Joshua 6:27 "So the Lord was with Joshua; and his fame was noised throughout all the country."*

# ORDER FORM

## ZOE MINISTRIES
4702 FARRAGUT ROAD • BROOKLYN, NY 11203 • (718) 282-2014

| TITLE | QTY | DONATION | TOTAL |
|-------|-----|----------|-------|
|  |  |  |  |
|  |  |  |  |
|  |  |  |  |
|  |  |  |  |
|  |  |  |  |
|  |  |  |  |
|  |  |  |  |
|  |  |  |  |
|  |  |  |  |

Guarantee: You may return any defective item within 90 days for replacement. All offers are subject to change without notice. Please allow 4 weeks for delivery. No COD orders accepted. Make checks payable to ZOE MINISTRIES.

| | |
|--|--|
| Subtotal | |
| Shipping | |
| Donation | |
| **TOTAL** | |

Name: _____ Phone _____

Address: _____

_____ Zip _____

**Payment by:** Check or Money Order (Payable to Zoe Ministries)
Visa • MasterCard • American Express • Discover

Card No.: _____ Exp. Date) _____

Signature (Required) _____